Printed in the United States
By Bookmasters

Who is the Holy Spirit; the third person of the Trinity? Several years ago, I attended a church service in which the speaker addressed the subject. He ended by saying that if we listen closely, we can hear that "still, small voice" speaking to us. He said we need to hear a fresh word from the Holy Spirit every day, just as Fresh Manna sustained the Israelites as they wandered the desert.

I wanted to hear God's voice, so I started asking and listening. As I sat with paper and pencil, thoughts came into my mind—words so clearly not from me; words of wisdom and encouragement; beautiful, godly words. I have recorded every word that has come to my spirit from God's Spirit. I have put a portion of these words into this book, as they are truly meant for God's church today. The Holy Spirit is in and around every believer, and He always speaks to those who will listen.

"However, when He, the Spirit of truth, has come, He will guide you into all truth; for He will not speak on His own authority, but whatever He hears He will speak; and He will tell you things to come" (John 16:13).

Kay Bonnell is currently a substitute teacher and artist. Her website, freshmannafromgod.com, shows many additional "love letters" and a number of her prints that have been made into greeting cards. She and her husband live in Mount Pleasant, Michigan.

U.S. $16.95

ISBN 978-1-4908-2300-

9 781490 823003

WESTBOW
PRESS
A DIVISION OF THOMAS NELSON
& ZONDERVAN

MY LEAF

BOOK ONE

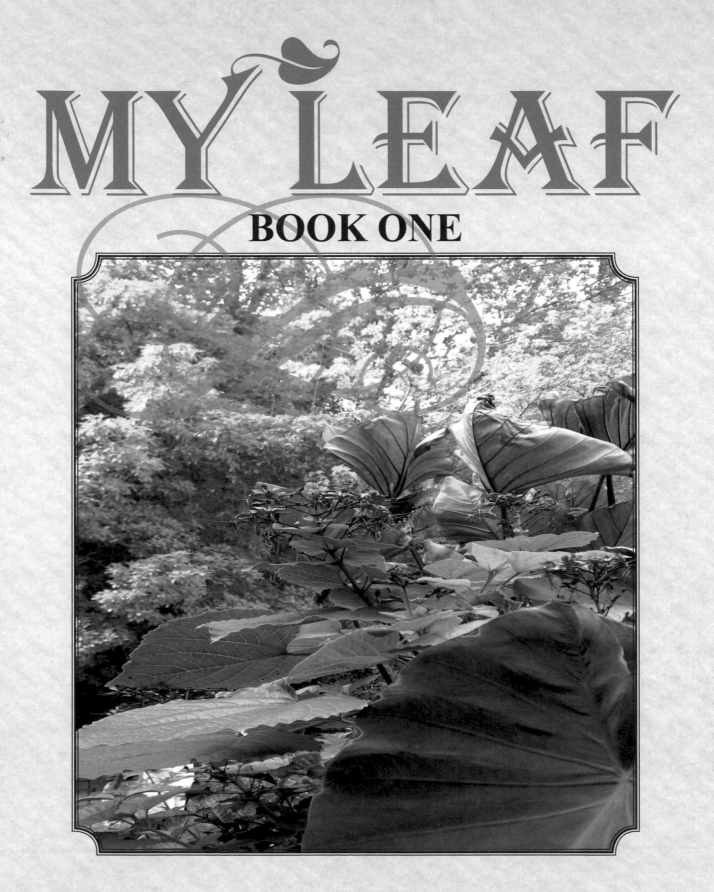

Written and Illustrated by

Maryam K Muhammad, MPH

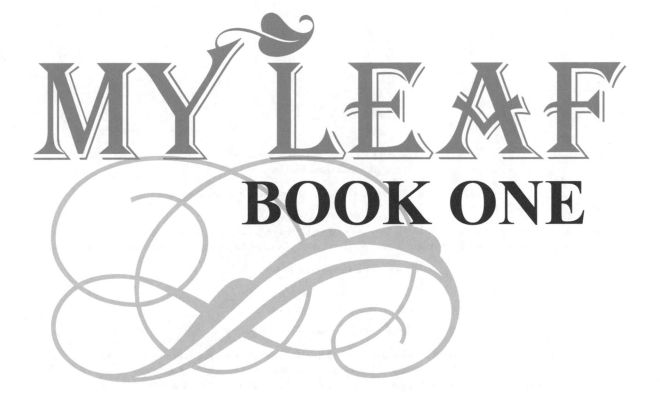

MY LEAF
BOOK ONE

Written and Illustrated by

Maryam K Muhammad, MPH

1st Editor, PharSide Coed Book Club
Maryam K. Muhammad, Avondale Estates, GA

Trafford rev. 5/16/2014

www.trafford.com

North America & international
toll-free: 1 888 232 4444 (USA & Canada)
fax: 812 355 4082

For my Beautiful Children:

Ashanti
Jameel
Nadirah
Najlah
And
Zafir

Without whom I would never have been
Able to slow down enough
To observe the flow of
The leaves
And
life.

ABOUT THE AUTHOR

Born to an ex-military and retired firefighter and an educator, Maryam K Muhammad was always reading and examining books and developing her writing skills and the skill of open expression. Due to her father's military background, Maryam traveled extensively. She loves visiting new places and experiencing new horizons.

As a child, Maryam would spend time in the yard playing with worms and examining the gardens her parents established. There were floral gardens and vegetable gardens in her yard. She would assist in the upkeep of the gardens and the yard.

After a hard day's work, Maryam, would sit on the porch and marvel at the bounties of life. One of her favorite was watching the flight of the leaves. The ability to soar and sail while going through the cycles of life amazed her.

Maryam Muhammad is an Epidemiologist. She studies trends of disease and loves traveling and exploring the world. She was told once by a childhood friend to make sure to, "take time and smell the roses." In doing so, she wanted to spend time in the environment and marvel at creation!

After acquiring her Bachelor's Degree in Family Sociology and Masters with a track II to PhD in Public Health Epidemiology, Maryam began working in Law Enforcement assisting in the community where she has been able to affect change in the lives of youth and adults of all ages.

Maryam currently resides in Georgia.

I AM GREEN.

I AM HANGING ON A BROWN TREE.

THE TREE IS TALL.

THE TREE IS IN THE DIRT.

THE DIRT IS BROWN.

THERE IS GRASS COMING OUT OF THE DIRT.

THE GRASS IS GREEN LIKE ME.

BEHIND THE GIRL ARE A LOT OF TREES.

I AM HANGING ON ONE OF THE TREES.

MY TREE IS FULL OF MANY LEAVES LIKE ME.

A TREE GIVES YOU SHADE.

THE GIRL IS PLAYING BALL IN THE SHADE.

THE GIRL IS PLAYING BALL BY MY TREE.

THE BIG BROTHER AND SISTER ARE WALKING.

THEY ARE ON THE WAY TO PICK UP THE GIRL BY MY TREE.

THE BROTHER AND SISTER ARE HAPPY.

THEY ARE WALKING PAST A TREE BUT IT IS NOT MINE.

I AM ON THE BRANCH OF MY TREE.

IT IS COOL AND WILL BE DARK SOON.

THERE WILL BE A LOT OF LIGHTS WHEN IT IS DARK.

THE BOY AND GIRLS MUST BE HOME BEFORE DARK.

IT IS DARK.

IT IS COOL.

THERE ARE BUGS WITH LIGHT ON MY LEAF NOW.

THERE IS A STREET LIGHT.

THE LIGHT IS YELLOW.

THERE ARE A LOT OF YELLOW LIGHTS.

DO YOU HEAR IT?

THAT NOISE IS LOUD.

THE SOUND IS "HOOT HOOT".

IT IS ON THE BRANCH BY ME.

IT IS AN OWL!

THE OWL IS BROWN.

SHE HAS BIG EYES.

DO YOU HEAR THE OWL ON
THE BRANCH BY ME?

LOOK!

THE OWL IS BROWN AND I AM
GREEN.

WHAT IS THAT?

IT HOPS.

IT IS GREEN LIKE ME.

IT IS ON THE LEAF OF THE TREE BY MY TREE.

IT IS MAKING A NOISE LIKE THIS, "RIBBIT RIBBIT."

IT IS A FROG!

THE FROG BLENDS IN WITH THE LEAF BECAUSE IT IS GREEN.

IT IS COOL OUTSIDE, NOW.

FALL IS APPROACHING.

I AM STILL HANGING ON MY
BRANCH.

SOME OF MY FAMILY HAVE
BLOWN AWAY.

I AM CHANGING TO
 ANOTHER COLOR.

THE SUN IS COMING OUT.

THE SUN IS YELLOW.

I AM NOT GREEN
ANYMORE.

I AM YELLOW.

I AM YELLOW LIKE THE
SUN NOW.

IT LOOKS LIKE AN EARLY
EVEINING COMING.

IT IS GETTING COOL

9

THE WIND IS BLOWING.

I AM TIRED AND SLEEPY.

I LOVE THE WAY I FEEL IN THE WIND.

THE WIND IS STRONG.

MY STEM IS NOT HOLDING ME ANYMORE.

I AM FLOWING IN THE WIND.

I AM FLOWING WITH THE WIND.

I AM AIRBORNE! WEEEEEEE!

NOW THE WIND HAS MOVED ME AWAY. WE ARE
DOWN SOUTH NOW AND IT IS NOT DARK.

WE ARE FAR, FAR AND AWAY FROM MY TREE.

I SEE THE MOUNTAIN.

I SEE ON TOP OF THE OTHER TREES.

I SEE A WATERFALL! IT IS STILL EARLY IN THE FALL DAY!

LOOK AT THE BUS!

THE BUS IS YELLOW.

THE BUS JUST PICKED UP THE CHILDREN FROM SCHOOL.

THE SCHOOL IS BIG!

THERE ARE NO LEAVES ON THE TREE.

FALL IS HERE.

LOOK AT THE DUCKS.

THE TEMPERATURE HAS DROPPED AND ALL
OF THE LEAVES ARE ON THE GROUND.

THE LEAVES ARE BROWN.

IT IS COLD.

IT IS WINTER.

IN THE SOUTH, THERE ARE DUCKS THAT PLAY IN THE WATER.

THE WIND HAS CARRIED ME TO THE CAR HERE IN THE NORTH.

I AM ON THE HOOD OF THE CAR.

THE CAR IS GREEN.

I WAS GREEN.

I AM TIRED AND WILL REST NOW ON THIS GREEN CAR.

WE ARE MOVING.

THE GREEN CAR IS MOVING.

I LOST MY GRIP ON THE GREEN CAR.

I AM IN THE AIR AGAIN.

THERE IS NO WIND.

I AM FALLING AGAIN.

I AM NOT GOING FAR.

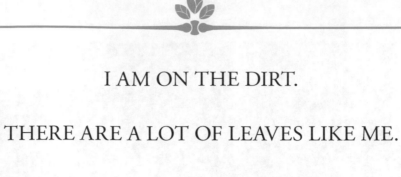

I AM ON THE DIRT.

THERE ARE A LOT OF LEAVES LIKE ME.

WE ARE ON THE COLD DIRT.

I AM BROWN NOW.

I AM THE SAME COLOR AS THE DIRT.

I AM GETTING VERY TIRED FROM MY TRAVELS THIS WEEK.

THE WIND IS PICKING UP.

IT IS DARK AND CLOUDY.

LOOK AT THE CLOUDS!   IT WILL RAIN TODAY.

IT RAINED LAST NIGHT AND WE MUST GO NOW.

LOOK! IT IS A GREEN AND BROWN RAKE.

SHE IS RAKING ALL OF US UP.

WE ARE GOING INTO A BROWN BAG.

THERE ARE A LOT OF BAGS.

WE ARE IN FRONT OF THE HOUSE.

WE ARE IN THE BAGS.

WE ARE BROWN.

WE ARE TOGETHER.

WE ARE GOING ON THE TRUCK IN THE MORNING.

WE ARE BY THE FENCE, WAITING TO BE RAKED UP.

GOODBYE MY BROWN LEAF.

I WAS GREEN.

I WAS YELLOW.

NOW I AM BROWN.

I AM NOW LEAVING WITH THE OTHER LEAVES.

I WILL BE BACK WHEN IT IS WARM.

WORD FIND

There are 19 words in this puzzle. Parents, you may copy this page for your child and make it into a game! See who can finish first. Have fun!

```
P  Q  B  E  S  R  S  Q  B  N  D  A  R  J  I
Q  M  E  F  I  E  S  D  E  I  G  L  B  H  P
S  R  P  B  S  A  A  E  D  E  R  F  U  Q  C
T  K  B  J  X  K  R  H  H  C  D  G  D  M
L  I  C  C  D  G  G  V  G  M  U  P  S  B  E
T  Y  V  U  M  H  E  R  D  O  Z  B  C  N  V
X  F  O  M  D  X  P  A  G  Z  R  W  O  A  G
R  W  O  Q  C  S  R  O  H  V  C  F  X  A  R
T  G  S  W  H  K  L  O  Z  W  O  G  A  S  M
O  E  O  D  I  W  O  L  L  E  Y  T  K  C  R
O  W  Y  P  L  M  P  O  P  X  H  O  X  U  A
L  E  R  H  D  L  I  G  H  T  N  O  F  B  F
T  R  I  D  R  H  U  O  F  B  F  H  L  E  S
X  Y  O  E  E  S  J  E  A  L  M  U  Y  I  G
W  I  N  D  N  E  T  U  J  R  A  W  Q  N  X
```

BIRD	BUGS	CAR
CHILDREN	DARK	DIRT
DUCKS	FLY	FROG
GRASS	GREEN	HOOT
LIGHT	OWL	RED
RIBBIT	TREE	WIND
YELLOW		

WORDS FOUND

So, how many words did you find???   List them below.

_____

_____

_____

_____

_____

_____

_____

_____

_____

_____

_____

_____

_____

_____

_____

_____

GREAT JOB!!

The picture of the tree on the previous page was taken in Madrid, Spain. Answer the following questions and Compare the tree to a tree in your yard or at your playground.

- How many branches do you see?

- What season is the picture showing?

- What color (s) are the leaves?

- Can you guess how old this tree is?

- What kind of tree do you have in your yard?

- How many branches are on the tree in your yard?

- What color are the leaves?

- Are the branches separated like the one in the picture?

- Do you climb your tree?

- Will you climb this tree if you were in Spain?

Write your answers here in this space:

_____

_____

_____

_____

_____

_____

_____

_____

_____

RESEARCH AND LIST

Please try to find these items. Where did you find them?

Brown Leaf   Found where:
Yellow Leaf   Found where:
Green Leaf   Found where:

Are there any other colors of leaves out there?

_____

What colors?

_____

Where did you find them?

_____

Take one of the Leaves that you found and measure the stem.   What is the measurement?

_____

Measure another one and record it's measurement.

_____

QUESTIONAIRE/NOTES

SKETCH AND LABEL
RESEARCH

On the next two pages, let's do some research together. Take one of your leaves and sketch it. After you sketch the front on this page and the back On the next page, label the leaf. You will need to research leaves to put down the vein (because leaves are vascular), xylem (brings water to the leaf), phloem (moves sap out of the leaf) and the stem.

FRONT/ADAXIAL (facing the stem-upperside)

BACK/ABAXIAL (FACING AWAY FROM THE STEM-UNDERNEATH)

So, Did you learn something about the biology of leaves? What makes the leaves change color?

Printed in the United States
by Baker & Taylor Publisher Services